E G G

Art Director: Rita Marshall
Book Design: Stephanie Blumenthal
Text Adapted and Edited from the French language by Kitty Benedict
Library of Congress Cataloging-in-Publication Data
Benedict, Kitty.
Egg/written by Andrienne Soutter-Perrot; adapted for the American reader
by Kitty Benedict; illustrated by Jocelyne Pache.
Summary: An introduction to the physical characteristics and
habits of the blackbird with emphasis on its egg.
ISBN 0-88682-565-2
1. Blackbirds—Juvenile literature. 2. Blackbirds—Eggs—Juvenile
literature. [1. Blackbirds. 2. Blackbirds—Eggs. 3. Birds.]
I. Pache, Jocelyne, ill. II. Soutter-Perrot, Andrienne. III. Title.
QL696.P2475B46   1992
598.8'81--dc20   92-15014

598.8
S

EG G

WRITTEN BY

ANDRIENNE SOUTTER-PERROT

ILLUSTRATED BY

JOCELYNE PACHE

CREATIVE EDUCATION

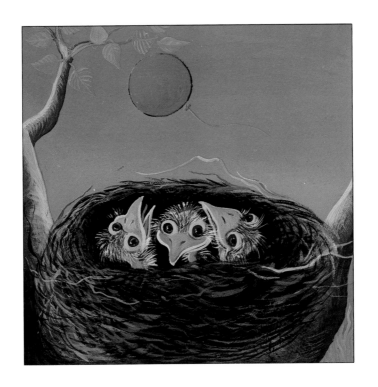

WHAT ARE THEY?

Look at the little blackbirds in their nest of twigs and grass. Are they all exactly alike?

When they are so little, they do all look alike. They have no feathers
on their bodies yet, and their wings are too short to be used for flying.

Fed and protected by their parents, the little blackbirds grow. They sprout gray feathers streaked with brown, and their wings become stronger.

As they grow older, little fledglings learn to fly and to find their own food.

Soon the birds are nearly as big as their parents. Their feathers have changed colors, and they are almost adults.

Do adult blackbirds all look alike? No, the females have gray-brown feathers and beaks, with light-colored breasts.

The males are bigger than the females. They have black feathers and bright yellow beaks.

HOW ARE THEY DIFFERENT?

Like all animals, blackbirds eat, breathe,
move about, and produce young.

Adult blackbirds have organs that help make babies. These are the reproductive organs.

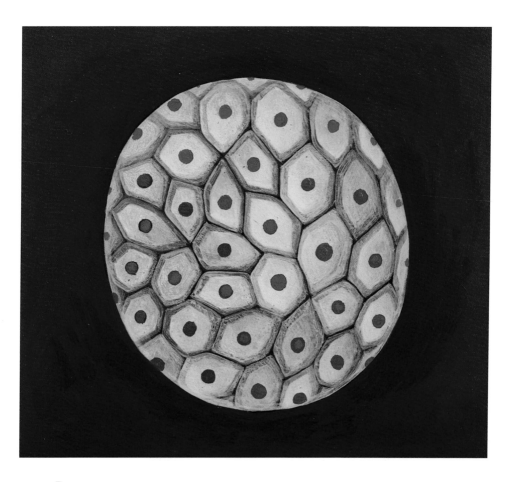

If you look at a piece of any organ through a microscope, you will
see tiny, irregular shapes set side by side. These are cells.

All organs are made up of cells. The reproductive organs, however, are also able to make special cells that reproduce life.

In the female blackbird these cells are called eggs. They are shaped like thick, round balls. Each is filled with a yellow yolk.

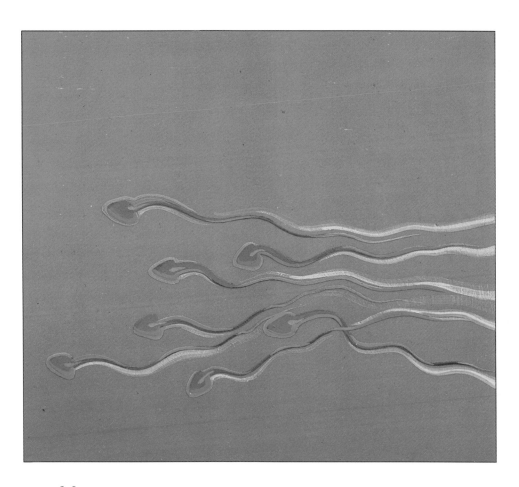

Male reproductive cells are called sperm. They are very small and
have long, wavy tails.

As you have seen, male and female blackbirds are not alike in their color, size, or reproductive organs.

HOW DO THEY REPRODUCE?

In the spring two blackbirds, one male and one female, build their nest in a sheltered place in a bush or thicket.

To mate, the female raises her beak and her tail, calling to the male
with little cries. The male answers her, then climbs on her back and
deposits a drop filled with sperm in her body.

Inside the female's body, hundreds of sperm swim toward the egg.

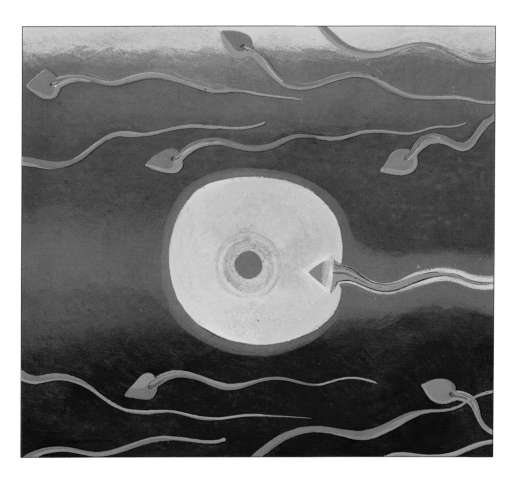

One of the sperm cells penetrates the egg, and the two cells become one. This union is called fertilization.

The fertilized egg is the beginning of a new baby blackbird.

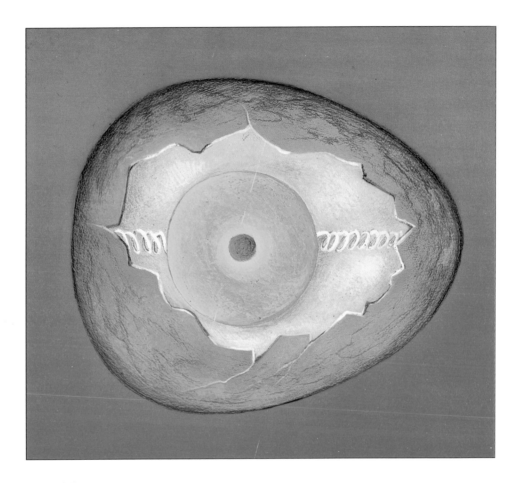

The egg is soon surrounded by a clear, sticky liquid and a hard shell.
Now the mother can lay the egg in her nest.

After she lays her eggs, the female keeps them warm beneath her body.

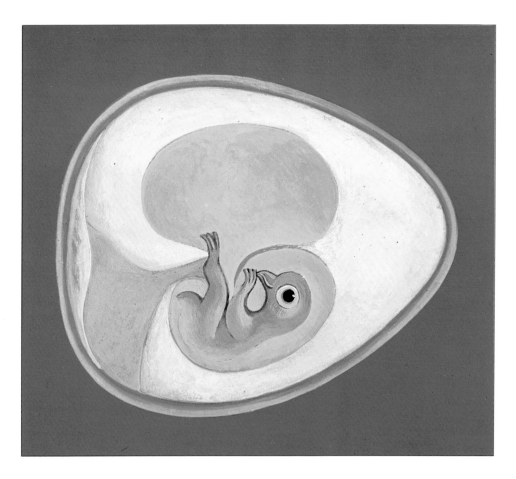

The egg's yellow yolk is food for the baby blackbird. The shell and the clear liquid protect the growing baby, and the mother's warmth keeps it alive so it can grow.

When the baby bird is big and strong enough, it breaks out of the shell with its beak and steps out. The egg has hatched!

DO OTHER ANIMALS MAKE EGGS?

All birds are hatched from eggs with shells.
But birds are not the only animals who
produce eggs.

All female animals make eggs. Every animal you know started out
as an egg.

Fish eggs are tiny. They hatch all by themselves in the water.
Turtles lay their eggs in the sand.

You can't see the eggs of a female dog, because they stay inside the mother's body. There they are kept warm and safe, until they are ready to be born as little puppies.

You, too, were once a tiny egg in your mother's body. It took nine months for you to grow into a baby.